What's Cooking?

Pauline Cartwright

Learning Media

Contents

1. The First Barbecue

Before **prehistoric** people knew about fire, they ate their food just the way they found it. So, who thought of using heat to cook food? Well, maybe someone found an animal that had been caught in a forest fire. The taste of the cooked meat must have been a surprise.

We'll never really know for sure – but one thing we do know is that people began to think of other ways of cooking their food by:

- roasting it over hot embers;
- wrapping it in wet leaves to steam cook it;
- putting hot stones in a pit to make a simple oven.

+ HEAT

How Food Cooks

Eggs, milk, and sugar mixed together aren't very interesting to eat. But if you heat them up, they will make pudding that tastes delicious. The heat changes the ingredients. They look and taste different. These changes can:

- make food taste better;
- make food easier to eat and to **digest**;
- give us different ways of enjoying food.

Here are three ways in which we use heat to cook our food:

1. The burner or oven heats up the liquid. The boiling liquid heats the food and cooks it. This is called convection.

2. The burner heats the pan. The pan heats the food and cooks it. This is called conduction.

3. The grill beams heat onto the food to cook it. This is called radiation.

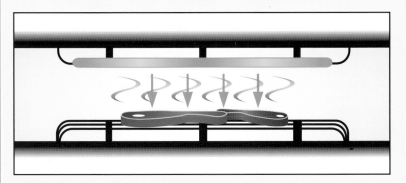

In this book, you can be the cook. There are some delicious recipes for you to try. They'll help you to understand how heat cooks food in different ways.
- Follow the steps carefully.
- Always ask an adult to help you.
- Wash your hands before you begin to cook.

2. You're in Hot Water

Using hot water to cook food is called "boiling." This is usually done in a saucepan over a burner. The burner heats the water in the pan, and the hot water cooks the food. Vegetables can be cooked like this.

Other foods that can be boiled are:
• poultry • meat • pasta • soups • sauces

Hot TIPS

- Water that's boiling can give you a bad burn, so be careful! Always ask an adult to help you.

- Don't leave a pot boiling. All the liquid might boil away. Then the food will stick to the pot and burn. Burned pots are very hard to clean!

- Some recipes say to let the food simmer. This means turning the heat down under the boiling pot so that the liquid stays hot but is moving only very gently.

- Use tongs or a spoon to lower food into boiling water. That will stop hot water splashing on you.

You're the Cook!

You can use boiling water to make this recipe. Follow the four easy steps. Remember – ask an adult to help you!

Easy-peasy Pasta

Ingredients

1 cup pasta spirals
1 tbsp. pasta sauce
1 tbsp. grated cheese
½ tsp. salt

1. Bring 4 cups of water to the boil.

2. Carefully put the pasta and salt into the boiling water. Boil for 5 minutes.

3. Drain the pasta, then pour it into a bowl.

If you want to make this recipe even tastier, add some diced chicken or some fresh, sliced tomatoes.

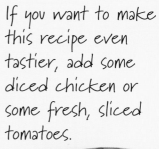

4. Stir the sauce into the pasta. Sprinkle the cheese on top.

3. Cookie Time

Cooking food in an oven, or on a hot surface like a **griddle**, is called "baking." Cookies can be baked in an oven. Biscuits can be baked in a heavy, hot pan.

Other foods that can be baked are:
• pastries • eggs • fruit • vegetables
• bread • cakes • meat

Hot TIPS

- Measure the ingredients carefully when you're baking.
- Heat the oven to the right temperature before you put the food inside. This helps the recipe to work properly.
- Don't open the oven door too often when the food is cooking. If you have to open the door, don't lean too close to it. It'll be hot in there!
- Use potholders to lift out trays or dishes.

You're the Cook!

Use an oven to bake these cookies.
Follow the six steps.
Remember – ask an
adult to help you!

Crispy Cookies

Ingredients

1 cup flour

1 cup coconut

1 cup oatmeal

1/2 cup sugar

1 tbsp. corn syrup

4 oz butter (cut into pieces)

1/4 cup milk

1/4 tsp. baking soda

1. Heat the oven to 300°F.

2. Stir the first four ingredients together in a bowl.

3. Heat the corn syrup, butter, and milk together in a small saucepan. When the butter has melted, add the baking soda.

4. Stir the liquid into the ingredients in the bowl.

5. Put teaspoonfuls onto oven trays. Press flat with a fork.

6. Bake for 15 minutes or until golden brown. Leave the cookies to cool on a rack.

You could stir 4 tablespoons of chocolate chips into the mixture before you put it onto the trays to cook. This recipe makes two trays of cookies.

4. Into the Frying Pan

Cooking food in hot vegetable oil, margarine, or butter is called "frying." Cooking food in a small amount of oil in a pan or skillet is called "shallow frying." Eggs can be cooked like this. Using a lot of oil in an electric fryer or saucepan is called "deep frying." French fries can be cooked like this.

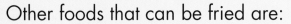

Other foods that can be fried are:
• meat • chicken • seafood • doughnuts
• vegetables

Hot TIPS

- If you are using oil, heat the oil before you put the food into the pan. If the oil begins to smoke, it's too hot. Never leave the room while food is frying.

- Put fried food on a paper towel to drain away the extra oil.

- Never put water (or wet food) into a hot frying pan. If you do, it will splatter and could burn you. Dry the food with a paper towel before you fry it.

You're the Cook!

Use a frying pan to cook this delicious fish. Follow the steps. Remember – ask an adult to help you!

Crumbed Fish

Ingredients

1 small **fillet** of fish

1 tbsp. flour

1 egg

2 tbsp. breadcrumbs

1 tbsp. butter

1 tbsp. oil

1. Dry the fish with a paper towel.

2. Roll the fish in the flour.

3. Beat the egg and dip the fish into it.

4. Roll the fish in the breadcrumbs.

5. Heat the oil and butter in the frying pan. When the butter is melted and mixed with the oil, put in the fish. When one side of the fish is browned, turn it and fry the other side.

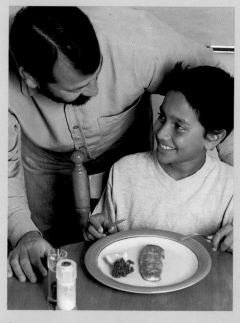

Squeeze some lemon juice over the fish. Eat it with a green salad.

5. Giving It a Grilling

Cooking food under a very high heat is called "broiling" or "grilling." You can also grill food over the flames of a barbecue.

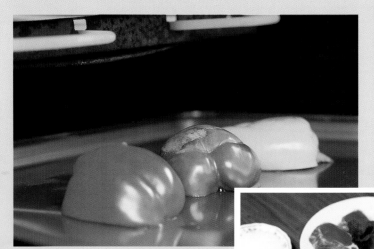

Some other foods that can be grilled are:
• vegetables • chicken
• meat • seafood

Hot TIPS

- *The grill should be heated to a high temperature before you put the food under it.*

- *If you are using an oven grill, always leave the door open a few inches.*

- *Oiling the grill on a barbecue first will stop food sticking to it.*

- *Use long tongs for lifting and turning food being grilled. Use potholders to lift out the cooking tray.*

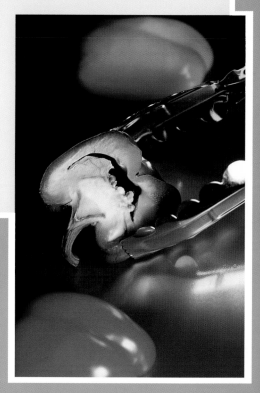

You can make this quick and easy snack under a grill. Follow these easy steps. Remember – ask an adult to help you!

Mini Pizzas

Ingredients

1 hamburger bun, cut into halves

ketchup

grated cheese

diced tomato

sliced sweet pepper

1. Turn on the grill and toast one side of the buns.

2. Turn the buns over and spread with ketchup.

3. Sprinkle with grated cheese.

4. Make a face with the tomato and sweet pepper.

5. Put the mini pizzas under the grill again until the cheese is bubbling.

Let the mini pizzas cool a little so that you don't burn your mouth. Grilled cheese can be very hot.

6. Crazy Waves

A microwave oven is a special kind of electric oven. It heats food by using special waves. The waves move the particles of food around and heat them  up. This happens a lot more quickly than in a regular electric or gas oven.

You can use a microwave oven to heat up leftovers quickly. Frozen food can be **thawed** quickly too. Most foods that can be boiled, baked, fried, or grilled can also be microwaved. But you need to read the recipe book carefully.

Hot TIPS

- Some microwaves are more powerful than others. Check the power level of the oven you're using. Higher power levels cook food faster than lower power levels.

- You can cook food in the dish you're going to serve it in. Check that the dish is "microwave safe."

- You can't put anything made of metal into a microwave – that includes twisties and plates with gold or silver patterns.

- Stirring or turning the food halfway through cooking helps it to cook properly.

- Cover the food to stop it splattering.

- Always let microwaved food cool a little before you eat it.

- Never turn on an empty microwave oven.

You're the Cook!

Use a microwave oven to make this recipe. Follow the four steps. Remember – ask an adult to help you!

Chocolate Pudding

Ingredients

2 tbsp. chocolate chips

2 tbsp. cornstarch

2 tsp. sugar

1/2 cup milk

1. Put all the ingredients into a bowl and stir them together.

2. Microwave the mixture for 1 minute on high power.

4. Microwave it for another minute on high power.

5. Let the pudding cool a little before you eat it.

3. Open the microwave and stir the mixture.

Add a chopped banana if you like.

Each recipe – except for the cookies – makes enough food for one person. You may want to cook for more people. Just multiply the amounts in the recipe by the number of people.

Glossary

(These words are printed in bold type the first time they appear in the book.)

digest: to break up food in the stomach so that it can be absorbed

fillet: a slice of fish or meat that has no bones

griddle: a flat pan or surface for cooking food

prehistoric: from the period in time before history was written down

thawed: when food that is frozen becomes unfrozen

Index